DEDICATION

To the parishioners and staff at St. Francis of Assisi
Parish, Raleigh, North Carolina... you are always
kind in the parking lot.

CONTENTS

From a Parish Priest

Poems by
Fr. Steve Kluge, O.F.M.

Grateful Leper Publishing

ISBN: 978-0-9763126-7-3

ACKNOWLEDGMENTS

A Word of Thanks...

To God... Who sustains my life.

To my family who have been the hook that begins many homilies...Yes, you are holy.

To my brother friars...For accepting me...Twice.

To the Poor Clares in Chesterfield, N.J....You are always home when I visit.

To the Saints of God on Long Beach Island, N.J....Through you Christ called me.

To the Saints of God in St. Francis Parish, Raleigh, N.C...Through you Christ healed me.

A Conclave of Cardinals

A conclave of cardinals
Gathered
On the snow vested ground
Eat
Fallen holly berries
While the world around them
Makes not a sound.

1

A Farmer Takes

A farmer takes
At least some credit
For sowing the seed.
Through word choices,
Which enter the unknownable
Soil of ear and heart,
We are all farmers,
And must take at least some credit or blame
No matter the harvest.

A Funereal Lament

Surrounded by satin sheets
On a California king sized bed,
Head propped on down pillows,
Windows draped in rich brocade,
Walk-in closet closed
Entombing Armani suits and shoes,
Chandelier dimmed so as not to strain the eyes,
Mozart muted on still spinning Bose,
The patient sleeps,
Breathing out
The patient sleeps
Breathing in
The patient slips
And stands in the grand great room
Naked and afraid.
And is asked the question,
"Whom did you bring?"

A, B, C...

Lord, I pray for:
Abundance overflowing
Beauty around me
Courage within me
Discernment guiding me
Encouragement coming towards me
Faithfulness within my heart
Gratitude on my lips
Hospitality given and received
Integrity of life
Justice towards others
Knowledge so as to teach
Love as an act of the will always
Mission so as to fulfill my life
Nobility at all times
Optimism no matter the circumstances
Patience towards others
Quiet as needed
Restfulness when harried
Solitude even when with others
Tolerance at least
Understanding those different from myself
Virtue growing despite my vices
Wisdom lived
Xanadu here on earth and heaven at last
Youthfulness no matter my age
Zest for living the life of Christ.

Advent

Arise from your slumber,
Get ready the feast.
With colored banners,
Prepare the halls and the walls.
Pick the tree
And decorate its branches
But leave off
Till later
The topping star
Or angel.
Let the celebration not be put off!
Our Hope has come
Wrapped in swaddling clothes.
Let joyful expectation give rise to action
As recognition of even-now-with –us Presence
Gives birth to wonder!
Still
Our Hope is yet to come
Wearing honor and glory,
Robed and crowned with the vulnerable power of
Love.
So as we wait
Let us do a bit of fasting before the feasting,
And decorate our festal robes with
Patient hope, and charity.
In this great already but not yet,
Let us permit the Advent preparations begin
For the great Christmas celebration.

A Psalm For Morning

Let my first thoughts be of thanks O Lord,
For You have led me safely through the night.
Let my next thoughts be of thanks O Lord,
For all You will give me throughout this day.
Let my speech be salted with thanks O Lord,
As I recognize Your abiding presence within all.
Let my actions be signs of thanks O Lord,
As without words I preach Your presence.
Let my last thoughts be of thanks O Lord,
And that will be enough.

A Psalm For Mid-Day

O Luminous Lord,
At zenith
Your sun
Seems to savor shadows
Shrinking
Pooling,
Sinking into ground made holy
Touched by unseen Presence.
Awareness now
Moves me
To pause,
To thank,
That through graced sustained,
I rise from shadow
Wrapped within Original Light
To walk once more on holy ground.

A Psalm For Evening

At the close of day,
YOU
Raise prayer
Within me:
Thanksgiving
Wraps round my contrite spirit
Since even sensing Your Shadow filled me with dread.
And though I often fled
Throughout this day,
YOU
Matched me step for step
And I could not run away.
From You,
Through You,
I ran and hid
Only to be found within the enclosure of Your
embrace.
Graced with unearned and undeserving grace.

A Riff on Genesis 32: 25-31

Of course,
When one wrestles with angels,
Secrets will be spilt,
Blood let,
Bones thrown out of joint.
Yet
Even in defeat,
Still cling,
For in the end
Blessings.

A Riff on St. Clare

If
You
Desire to know if
Holiness grows within you,
Then,
Gaze at your feet and
Consider where they take you.
Gaze at your hands and
Consider if they heal or hurt.
Gaze at your tongue and
Consider the effects of your words.
Contemplate the
Desires of your heart.
And if one, or at best all,
Imitate
Christ,
Then you know that
Holiness
Grows within you.

A Riff on the Magnificat: Luke 1:46-55

*We make God visible in the world
And our spirits are filled with joy for God is the
Creator, Redeemer, and Sustainer of our life.
In our lowliness, God looks upon us and calls us
friend, daughter, son and so all will come to know that
we are forever blessed.
God Your holiness is shown to us in all the wonderful
ways you love us.
Your mercy causes us to stand up and take notice.
Your love for us confuses the proud in the hardness of
their hearts.
Your love for us raise us to places of honor and respect
while those now mighty are humbled.
Your love and acceptance satisfies our deepest hungers,
while those now filled with riches and power find
themselves hungry.
O Lord, remember Your promise to be with us all the
days of our life.*

An Opened Door

The heart is
An opened door
Through which the world
Wounded by sin and
Grace,
Unbidden enters
Received with a curious
Unequal mixture of
Hostility and hospitality.

At Prayer

Sometimes
My heart's mind is mosquito filled,
Or worse,
Becomes a hive of stinging bees.
Though not often,
Grace creates translucent space
Filled with flickering fireflies
Telling of Divine insight
And I am satisfied.

At the Start of Day

At the start of day,
May I remember:
Christ heals the wounded,
Christ forgives the sinner,
Christ feeds the hungry,
Christ refreshes the thirsty,
Christ remembers the forgotten,
Christ finds the lost,
Christ clothes the naked,
Christ comforts the sorrowing,
Christ companions the lonely,
Through me
And all of us called Church.
For having been baptized into Christ
So as to become Christ,
And Spirit filled,
The incarnation
And saving mission
Goes on,
and on,
And on.

Mass on Death Row

Before my arrival
At the storage room
Soon to be made an ante-room of heaven,
But heaven nonetheless,
They are gathered.
There is nothing else for them to do.
Though not a feast of martyrs, they are
Dressed in jumpsuits
Blood red;
So as to call to mind a blood spilt past
Or of blood- letting yet to come?
Greeted
With fist bumps or shoulders touching,
Around a wobbly table made altar
Symbol of our wobbly lives, we are
Seated
Side by side by side, and
Sign ourselves
As already crucified,
Dead, and dying.
Marked with the red blood of a Savior
Giving strength to a fragile hope
In one day Rising.
Heard Word
Becomes question
And pause for reflection,
Birthing

From condemned lips
Prayers, pleas, and supplications
Not for themselves, but
For families near and far
Afflicted still by nightmare's touch.
When at last
The blessing,
The breaking,
The taking and the eating,
The outpouring and the drinking,
The shyly observed feasting
Makes incarcerated men walking tabernacles.
With a final blessing
These men,
My brothers,
Are led back
Into the hell of prison hall
Carrying the Christ
Once again condemned,
Or freely choosing,
To live on death row.

Come Away With Me

Come away with Me.
Whisper you dreams and sorrows.
I will hide them,
Heal them,
Keep them safe
Until the Bright Tomorrow.

Confetior Deo

Though I try to tread gently,
My feet still bend and break
The slender reed,
Or displace
The desert dust.
My mouth grunts gripes
While gracious gratitude chokes in
my throat.
Hands grab
At this world's goods,
Giving far less than receiving.
My body in foggy weather
Cleaves those wrap around clouds
And on sunny days,
My shadow shades flowers
Longing for the sun.
Confetior Deo Omnipotente,
That the good that I would do,
Could do and should do,
Everyday,
I do not.

Credo

I give You my heart O God,
That I may love You first
And above all my other loves.
To You I give my feet:
Take me where You will.
To You I give my hands:
Use them to heal.
To You I give my mouth:
Let me speak blessings.
To You I give my nose:
Fill it with the fragrance of Your holy and priestly
people.
To You I give my eyes:
Let me see Your sacredness surrounding all.
To You I give my mind:
So at last,
Overwhelmed by Your gift of holy contemplation
I may begin to follow in the footsteps of Your Son.

Crumbs and Flakes

Let's begin to celebrate,
Not only the bread and fish
Taken, blessed and eaten,
But
The tenderly gathered
And counted leftovers:
Sacramental nonetheless,
The crumbs and flakes,
Reminders and remainders
Of the once eaten Feast.

Do Those Who Stand

Do those who stand
With perfect posture,
Chest out,
Shoulders back
And head held high,
Know
That they too are not yet
What
They shall be?
Or has the hope
Between what is
And what ever shall be
Been fulfilled for them?
And if so,
What about the hope for me?

Another Easter Dawning
(with thanks to Melissa Misko-Blanton)

Each morning Lord,
You gift me
With the Grace to be
Reborn at breakfast.
Another Easter dawning.
And I feast
On the question,
"Who would You have me be this day?"

Firefly

I held a flickering
Firefly
In my hand.
But when momentarily
Distracted
By the darkness,
I didn't feel it fly
Away.

From Trembling Lips

From trembling lips,
Prophets words
Bring dread.
Choose,
To live a life of blessing
Or cursing.
A lifetime of choices
Pull back a curtain
Allowing us to see
Who we are becoming
And who we will remain
For all eternity.

Grace Before Meals

Loving God,
We thank you for this food.
Bless it and the many hands from which it has been
received,
So that we may better serve Your holy and priestly
people.

Grace is Wild

Grace is wild:
A shimmering personal thing
That transforms the harshest winter
Into eternal spring.

God as Tree

God as Tree
Root
Trunk
Branch
A Trinity of sorts
And we
The leaves of course.

God's home

God's home is not
Some far off place,
Unreachable mountain top,
Not hidden in the sea.
God's home is
Among us,
Within us,
And so we find our home in God.

I Live Enclosed

I live enclosed
Between
Candles and candies.
Turned at times toward one
Or the other.
Yet while turned,
Called
Not to deny,
But to recognize and rejoice
In the light of one
And the sweet fragrance of the other.

I Spent a Great Deal of Time Today

I spent a great deal of time today
Counting my blessings.
Four hundred-ninety to be exact…
Oh,
I forgot one.

Ignore the Sun

Ignore the sun
At your own peril.
But the moon
Waxes and wanes unnoticed
By most
Yet still reflects
A gentle light
In the darkness
Of the still and holy
Night.

In the Cool Part of the Day

In the cool part of the day,
Walk through the Creator's own cathedral
With unbound feet,
For this is holy ground.
Feel the grass tickle your toes,
Inhale the sweet perfumed praise of
Lilac, violet, and wild red rose.
Listen to the secret hymns of sparrow
Crow and jay.
Gaze upon deer and fawn
As they sleep amid the light of day.
Consider the hawk's easy flight
As upon thermals of air they glide.
Slowly sip and taste
Then deeply contemplate the too sweet nectar of honey
suckle on the vine,
Come to know that
All is Bread and all is Wine
For all who hallow the Creator Divine.

Is it the Tree

*Is it the tree
That grasps
The last of the leaves,
Or
The leaf that clings
As the wintry winds blow?*

It is Into This Bit of Dust

It is into this bit of dust,
This clay,
This shallow, hardened
Rocky soil,
But still
A little rich,
In which
Through water,
Word and Spirit,
You plant Yourself as seed.
It is I,
Not You,
Who is a parable of paradox.

I See Assisi: A Collection of Poetry

1. First View

O city set upon a hill side,
Through cloudy veil
And early evening light,
Your golden pink stones call to me-
COME,
Enter past my walls
And see in children present
Your parent's smile and eyes.
Down ancient alleyways
Their voices still echo:
Crying,
Laughing,
Singing-
Hoping,
Dreaming,
Yielding,
Building a vision not clearly seen,
Of openness embracing all,
Mountain high and valley deep.

2. Cheisa Nova

Birth place of a saint,
So simple
Now marbleized.
Stony veins create a stony heart
Of altar's edge.
But water flowing breaks the rock,
And Love will melt the sinner's heart.

3. San Ruffino

Carved in stone
A shallow bowl
Holds water made holy through prayer.
This makes and marks the spot
Of Spirit's first intruding.

4. San Damiano (Francis)

"The stone", Francis,
"The stone
See the stone.
Touch it and lift it up,
Carry it to its' rightful place.
If need be,
Cut and carve the jagged edges
So that stone and mortar may embrace."
    SAN DAMIANO (CLARE)
Embrace me
Within these hallowed walls

Built of sweat and tears and stone.
The start of life again,
But not for me alone.

5. Santa Chiara

I do not want the stony walls,
Nor frescoes newly painted.
I will not go to distant hills
Nor sweet vale below.
I do not want eternal praise
From people through the ages.
But this I choose:
To be held in loving gaze
By YOUR sublime and holy face.
To be considered poor enough to receive YOUR
beneficence,
To contemplate my life and be enclosed within YOUR
will.
To imitate YOUR outstretched arms and pierced
hands
Mean more to me than all the wealth in all the lands.
And this,
For me is holy poverty.

6. The Portiuncola

Here in this place,
I make my yes.
To be servant-not master,
To wash the feet of brother and sister,
To cast no judgement,

To work and pray,
To live each passing day in gratitude.
Here,
In this my little 'yes'
I make my home,
Humbly knowing
That YOU have first said 'yes' to me.

7. La Maddelana

Tender care is needed here-
Dusty and overlooked
The walls cry.
The people sigh
For the city no longer theirs.
But within these walls
Compassion
First finds a home.

8. Rivo Torto

Twigs and stone
Did not build the hut-
But Daring,
Compassion,
And Conviction.
The stream runs its' course
And a seed is planted
By humble men with grateful hearts.

9. La Verna

How grand a mystery,
To shroud a mountain gray and white
And then to pierce the clouds
With morning light.
To cause the trees to grow
To make them loose their leaves
When autumnal winds do blow.
How grand a love
To touch the earth
Through woman's flesh and human birth.
To open arms upon a cross
To rend your heart so Spirit leaves
Throughout the world to go.
Our God bends low
To kiss a heart,
And pierce the hands and feet
Of one who heard and lived the call
Of Love's grand Mystery.

10. Carceri

While Assisi sleeps
Blanketed by clouds and mist,
Up, up, up we go
To where on mossy mattresses
Stone pillows lay silent.
It is here
That prayer begins,
Takes root
And starts to grow.

11. Santa Maria Maggiore

Naked,
I stand in front of my parents.
Naked,
I stand in front of my friends.
Naked,
I stand in front of prelate and court.
Naked,
I stand in front of God.
…and I am unafraid and not ashamed.

12. Basilica San Francesco

Sleep was not mine
While I was alive.
Nor does it come to me in death.
Placed high above the earth,
On stony bed
With a stony pillow for my head,
Imprisoned by an iron grate
I see the throngs
And hear their pleas
For pardon, love and charity.
But none of this was my intent.
And this
At last,
Is poverty.

13. Greccio

To the mountain,
But not its peak
Love must be remembered.
Wood and stone make a stable,
People,
Not statues sing
And all creation joins the chorus.
Love has come to life!

14. Lateran

The Seat and Center:
Ancient doors of bronze now patina green
Locked
Within a field watered by martyrs blood.
To rebuild or shore up?
To renew or tear down?
To unlock the doors!

It Seems That I Have Seized

It seems that I have seized
All of Your low-hanging fruit.
Yet Your Spirit
Invites me
Compels me
To write once more
Of Mystery.
So bend lower
Come closer
Since I cannot reach to even touch
Unless Your Spirit assists me.

Leaves are Birthed

Our lives are like leaves.
Birthed
In bound buds turned inward
Bathed by sun's warmth and
Baptized by spring rains
Gentle moving breezes invite
Be opened.
Slowly bursting forth
While wrapped in garments of green
Feasting on sunlight,
Washing in rains;
Waltzing with the summer's breeze
To music divine
Unheard by human ears.
But with the cooling of the daylight
While autumnal winds blow,
It is then in the dying
All the hidden
Multi-colored glory
Can finally be seen
And the holding on becomes
A letting go.

Manifest Yourself

Manifest Yourself
To me
O God,
Father, Son, and Spirit,
In all Your Poverty
So that I may see
It it's truly
You
I want and
Not all You have for me.

Meditation on St. Joseph

Were you filled with awe
Or something else,
When you saw
An angel sent to wash away your doubts?
Yet how surprised you must have been
To find no place to stay in Bethlehem,
Your ancestral town still filled
With distant relatives.
Did dread and fear fill your heart
As once again an angel sent
Instructing you to rouse your family and depart?
You must have cried
And screamed your grief
At the news that all those babies died.
Did you at last,
trust the angelic message
Commanding your return to land both holy and
hostile?
When at last your life was done,
No angel came for you.
You had had enough of angels
And what it is they have to say.
But your beloved foster Son
Came to lead you on the way.

My Sister Moon

My Sister Moon
Has no light of her own,
Yet shines
Due to the generosity of
Our Brother Sun.

Mystics speak of the GLORY of God:

Mystics speak of the GLORY of God:
As if GLORY
Were written in all caps
In big, bold font
And shouted at creation.
But I am not a mystic.
I speak of God's glory
Whispered from within.
Creation's glory a shallow breath,
Given and received between
Creator and creature now set free.
Bushes everywhere,
Softly crackling with Spirit's flames
While only one is still enough to hear
Burning branches moan
Unconsumed.
The poor, the widow, the stranger,
Weep under the weight of indifference
With only prophets words to bind up wounds.
An angel's apparition
And blessed conversation
Cloak
That most Divine moment of impregnation.
While nine months later
Night shrouds a unique birth
While the heavenly hosts sing full throated

GLORIAS

To out shout the screams and panted breaths of a
virginal birth.
Temple veils tear
So we do not see a mother's tears
Nor hear sighs
Mingle with her crucified son's blood.
Three days later,
Stone slides away from borrowed tomb
When something more than resuscitation,
Resurrection:
Creation made new
In silent wonder surfaces.
Now even angles are struck dumb
While creation swoons
And sighs the deepest sigh,
This time in relief.

One November Morning

One November morning,
The air damp and chilled,
I stood silent and still
Amid the oak, the elm, the poplar
And watched
Awestruck
As red, orange, and yellow tears
Floated from denuding branches
And with an almost silent rustle,
Grew the great multi- colored carpet at my feet.

Open me Lord

Open me Lord.
I have closed my heart to a Wild God,
And have fashioned from my own desires a
Domesticated deity.
Open me Lord.
I have stopped my ears from hearing
Your world turning Word
And have written my own lyrics
That lull me to sleepwalk through life.
Open me Lord.
I have closed my eyes to
Ever expanding Wonder
And am content to see
Nothing but monotony surrounding me.
I surrender.
So open me Lord.
Bid me come out of
The pit that I have dug,
So that united with Your holy and priestly people
I can once again and
Truly live.

Poets and Pray-ers

Poets and pray-ers
Carry the same millstone.
Light as a pillow case filled with eider down
But a millstone nonetheless.
Pray-ers and poets,
Like two oxen yoked,
Plod on in search of a word
That will articulate the unseen within
All that is seen;
Brighten the gloom
Or dim the too bright light;
Disclose the secrets of the soul
And heal the hurts of the Divine and human heart.
Poets and pray-ers
Pregnant with words not fully formed
Wait like tigers stalking prey
To loose the tongue,
Unleash the pen,
To let the feathers fly wherever they may.

Psalm 1

*The destiny for those who keep Your law is one of
blessedness,
While the wicked condemn themselves.
I open myself to daily following Your path,
And this brings joy to my being,
I am like a willow planted near a spring of living
water.
Though the winds turn cold,
Its open leaves never wither and die.
But the wicked are like trees in the desert.
With no water to refresh them,
They grow weak,
Their leaves, closed, soon wither and die,
Driven off by the hot howling winds.
When judgement comes,
The wicked will not survive,
They have made themselves a closed ruin,
And will find no room in the assembly of the faithful.
But the just have opened themselves to receive the
Lord's care,
And this care will be for them from eternity to
eternity.*

Psalm 3

I have many enemies, Lord.
Many people are against me.
Many say "God will not save him."
But You O Lord wrap me in Your Protection;
You are my Glory.
I hold my head high, I am unbowed.
With You beside me I am not afraid.
At night I am weary and sleepy,
And the Lord covers me with a blanket of protection.
In the morning I rise refreshed
For the Lord has saved me through the night.
Even if thousands of enemies surround me I will not
be afraid.
Come to me Lord! Save me O God!
You will defeat all of my enemies;
They will no longer speak threats against me.
Safety and peace are blessings of the Lord.

Psalm 4

Answer my questions Lord.
When troubled and lost, clear a path for me.
Bless me by hearing my prayers.
God asks how long will we mock Him,
Dishonor Him by living dishonest lives and chasing
after dust.
But for those whose lives are filled with truth and
integrity,
The Lord works wonders
And hears their prayers.
So stand before God filled with fear and awe,
Be truthful and contemplate Him in silence.
Offer your life as a sacrifice to God.
Many pray to have good times in order to see the light
of Your face.
But to me You have given a more abundant joy.
And when the time comes,
I will lie down and sleep in peace.
For You Lord are my security.

Psalm 6

Don't be disappointed with me Lord,
Don't let Your punishments be done in anger
Since You have created me out of dust.
I am weak,
And my body trembles with fear because of Your
silence.
Even my soul is burdened with terror,
As I wait, and wait and wait for You to answer my
prayer.
Once again look upon me,
Save me for I am drowning.
You are Mercy.
Rescue me from the waves of anxiety and death that
wash over me.
I am so tired of sighing,
At night I cry into my pillow,
In the day my chair is soaked from my weeping.
My eyes are red and swollen from sorrow
I am worn out from seeing all of my enemies.
I cry aloud, "Get away from me all who curse me and
would do me
harm!"
But then the Lord sees my tears
And hears my crying.
The Lord avenges me
And my enemies flee,
They themselves are now afraid and disgraced,
Running and falling away in shame.

Psalm 8

Creator God,
God of the universe,
Father God, Mother God of us all,
My God,
I am filled with awe when I think of You,
For You are greater than all Your works,
Yet fit Your love within all You have made,
And show Yourself even in the smallness and
helplessness of babies.
Even then, Your enemies are not victorious.
When I look upon everything that can be seen,
And all that remains unseen,
Created by the comingling of Your Breath and Word,
I sigh.
Who are We, O Lord?
Who are You that You care for us?
Who am I that You care for me?
Yet You created us a little less than Yourself,
And offer us crown of glory and honor.
You trust us to rule in Your name,
Over every work of Your hands.
Creation in all its forms You put beneath our feet
And ask us to tread lightly.
How wonderful!
How trusting!
How awe inspiring are You O Lord!

Psalm 11

When afraid,
I turn to the lord for safety,
So how can you say to me
"Like a bird fly away and hide."
Even though my enemies hide themselves in the dark,
Waiting to shoot at me,
When all around me seems to be falling apart
What can i do but turn to you o lord.
The lord is greater than any of us,
The lord is mightier than all of us,
The lord keeps careful watch over us.
We are all of us tested,
So that we can see who we are.
The good as well as the bad are tested.
The lord hates violence
And rains down wrath upon the wrathful
Filling them up with the rotten fruit of their evil
actions.
But to those who do good,
To those whose act with justice and mercy,
God will be for them just and merciful.

Psalm 24

The earth and all that is created belongs to the Lord.
Everyone, each in their own way, belongs to God.
No matter how unsteady our world,
God gives us security.
But how can I go to the Lord's place?
How can I stand in God's presence?
My heart and my hands are not pure,
My desires run rampant
And sometimes I wish my neighbor ill.
Yet the Lord enters into the world,
His glory fills the universe.
The Lord is powerful and courageous,
Loving and healing and humble.
Permit the Lord to enter into your heart,
Be filled with His glory,
And He will carry you into His holy place.

Psalm 32

God brings forgiveness of sin,
A cleansing of guilt and deceit,
And thus I am blessed by the LORD.
Sin silence broke my bones,
In pain and loneliness I groaned and moaned.
Your Hand, heavy with compassion,
Was gently laid upon me,
And my strength left me as if I were in the desert in
the summer.
My parched lips confessed my sin to You,
I said, "I have sinned against You, O LORD,"
And my sin vanished like fog in the light of your
compassion.
Learn that neither sin, nor guilt, nor distress should
stop prayer.
Though surrounded by dangers,
I am safe within Your protective presence.
The LORD instructs me how to live,
And gives me footprints in which to place my feet,
Your advice and watchful eye
Stops my hindering anger,
And I come to You once more.
The wicked have many sorrows,
But to those who trust You LORD,
You surround with LOVE.
So be glad and rejoice all you who are clean of heart,
For the LORD, the Most High, is with you and has
touched you.

Psalm 46

In times of trouble,
When the world may shake,
Though the sea may rage,
Thought the mountains fall or erupt,
Though nations war against each other,
Though kingdoms collapse,
I turn to God: my help, my refuge,
The One who gives me strength.
For God indeed dwells within the heart of creation,
And His Word makes the heart brave:
God is with us,
And His work is peace.
Calm down,
Calm down,
God is God and is still active in our world.

Psalm 63

My Lord and My God,
How I thirst for You here in this world.
I thirst not for water,
But for You.
My body cries out not for food,
But for You.
I have caught glimpses of Your Glory
Within Your Assembly.
Your Love is Life giving,
O How can I praise You?
With hands and voice I will praise You,
For I remember You during the day,
And in the night,
When in the deepest sleep,
You are, even then, my Helper and Sustainer.
From the heat of day You shade me,
You illumine my darkest night.
With a tight tenderness,
You grip my hand,
And gently lead me from all harm.
So let me rejoice in You
My God and My Guide.

Psalm 70

LORD, I am at my wits end,
And so I turn to you for rescue and help.
Because of Your love for me, help me
Be my rescuer.
Confuse those who would shame me and ruin me.
Let my enemies themselves be shamed and defeated.
Reward those who turn and seek YOU,
Let them rejoice and be glad in YOUR saving help.
I am here, afflicted and poor,
Humbled,
Humiliated,
And preyed upon.
My Helper and Deliverer,
Make YOUR presence known to me.
Do not delay O my VICTOR,
And I will sing YOUR praises, all the days of my
life.

Psalm 71

I place myself in YOU LORD,
My Refuge,
Let me not be shamed or disgraced.
As JUSTICE,
Be my RESCUER and DELIVERER,
The ONE WHO LISTENS and SAVES,
MY ROCK of REFUGE,
MY SECURE STRONGHOLD,
MY FORTRESS.
My GOD,
From the vain power of the wicked and the violent,
Rescue and Save me.
Once again,
As I have since my youth,
I hope and place my trust in YOU, LORD.
From within my mother's womb,
Before the day of my birth,
YOU have strengthened me
And so my hope in you never grows weak.
Many think I am a display of YOUR anger,
But still I place my trust in YOU
Singing praises of Your glory every day and in every
circumstance.
Now that I am old,
Do not discard me.
As I become weak,
Do not abandon and forget me.
My enemies speak against me,

They watch and plot against me.
They say, "GOD has abandoned that one.
So let us seize him,
For GOD will not rescue him."
GOD,
Be close to me and quickly help me.
Shame those who would harm me,
Cover them with YOUR anger.
I will always hope in YOU
I will sing YOUR praise,
Though too numerous to count,
I will speak of YOUR wonderful deeds of
deliverance,
And Your mighty works of Divine Justice.
YOU have been my Teacher since my youth,
Now that I am old and gray,
Stay with me O GOD.
To those yet unborn,
And to those in the heights of heaven,
Let my life be a witness of YOUR Mighty Power
and Justice.
YOU have no equal,
DIVINE WORKER OF WONDERS.
Though often afflicted,
YOU revive me,
From the chaos,
YOU raise me up,
Restore my honor,
And give me Comfort,
So that in song I may praise YOU, my GOD,
The HOLY ONE of Israel,
Both old and new.
Those who would disgrace me will themselves be
disgraced,

And I will once again shout for joy,
For YOU have redeemed me.

Psalm 93

Majestic robes clothe the LORD Who creates and governs;
Whose Word and Wisdom are shown throughout the universe.
The Lord is eternal.
Through floods and drought,
Famine and abundance,
Sickness and health,
The LORD reigns forever.
More mighty than any evil or calamity that befalls us,
The Lord is alway loving,
And clothes His people with His own holiness
Forever and ever. Amen. Alleluia.

Psalm 98

Everyone come out from hiding,
Dance, sing and celebrate!
With song and movement
Stand before the Lord!
Let the earth,
The universe with all its' wonders
Stand in joy before the Lord
Who is our loving Judge.
The Lord's verdict is "Holiness";
His truth is that we are loved.

Psalm 102

Hear my prayer for help, O God.
Do not turn away.
Bend low
So that you can hear my whispered cries
For I am in distress.
My days are filled with troubles and anxieties.
Even my body rebels against me.
My muscles ache,
My bones crack,
My teeth stand on edge.
I am like a zombie
Neither dead nor alive.
I sleep walk through the day,
And lie awake at night.
My enemies are within and without.
I have nowhere to hide.
I am hungry,
But food does not satisfy.
Water does not quench my thirst.
So at last I turn to You, O Lord,
Who are always with me.
O Eternal Listener: You answer me.
O Place of Safety: You hide me.
O Source of Peace: You calm me.
O Divine Physician: You heal me.
You give me Life,
And I am Your servant,

Entrusted to speak of all that You have done for me.
And so I speak,
I sing of Your Love and Concern
To all those You place before me.

Psalm 103

With all that I am,
I will bless You,
I will thank You,
I will give You praise, O Lord.
May I live always remembering Your mercies:
Forgiveness,
Well- being,
Freedom,
Lovingkindness and Compassion.
You crown me,
And I am royal.
You are Truth,
You show us the Way to Life,
And when we fall short
You are Patience and Pardon.
You,
The Summit of All Perfections,
Reach out to us,
And our transgressions and guilt,
You wash away.
You,
O Perfectly Loving Parent,
Know that we are wayward children.
Small and weak,
Yet Your Love for us is Absolute and Eternal.
So small and weak are we,
Like snow,

Whose beauty fades in the presence of the sun.
Yet
You know us,
For You have made us,
Fashioned us to Youself.
You have gifted us with eternity
So that the memory of all You have done
will last from everlasting to everlasting.
So with all that I am,
I will bless You,
I will thank You,
With all that I ever shall be,
I will give You praise, O Lord
And I will live always remembering Your Mercies.

Psalm 111

While my words fail,
And my thoughts cannot fully comprehend,
Yet I will offer praise and thanks.
But not alone
O Lord,
Not alone.
For You have surrounded me with a cloud of
witnesses
Who remember all Your majestic deeds,
And sing in some new way of Your Glory.
O Worker of Wonders,
May I never forget You,
But may I spend the length of my days
Caught up in participation of Your great Self Gift.

Psalm 113

Let all those who serve the LORD give praise and
blessings!
Praise the LORD Who is not bound by time,
Praise the LORD Who is not tied to one place.
The LORD is greater, mightier, higher than any
nation;
Above all that ever was, is now, or ever shall be.
No one or no thing is like the LORD Who sees
everything,
And lovingly holds all divinely created things in being.

Those persons on the margins,
Those shunned by society,
Those who know they are poor and needy,
Those without a place,
The LORD raises up and embraces;
Treating them like royalty.
The LORD makes for them a palace within God's
Self.
And like a mother,
Makes them Daughters and Sons
Through a share in the gift of the LORD'S own
Divine life.

Gives us Divine Life.

Psalm 126

Did you forget me O God?
Why was your back turned against me?
But now You remember me
And once again Your face is turned toward me.
Because of the joy you give me,
I sing and shout with glee,
Together, You and I, dance.
Now everyone can see that You remember me,
The wonderful deeds You have done for me.
Like a once dried river bed
I now overflow with Your blessings.
Tears filled with sadness,
Are now signs of joy.
My heavy burdens are now lighter than air,
And the desperate deeds planted in despair
Have flowered into an abundance of hope.

Psalm 139

How intimately You know me O God.
Before I knew myself,
You knew me,
And into Your plans You made a place for me,
Gifting me with all that I need to fulfill Your Good
Will for me.

I cannot argue Your love for me
That You created me according to Your Own Design.
Unique and so profoundly loved
You created me,
And I cannot comprehend it.
With Your love and tenderness I have being,
Gifts not earned,
And never to be lost.

Your gifts to me fascinate me and cause me to tremble.
Your presence clothes me.
And from the deepest part of myself,
You, Creative Love,
Hug and caress me.
Yet, not knowing why,
I squirm and cry for release.
And still You hold my whole unholy self
Close,
Horizon like.
Closer than I am to myself.

Gift me once more.
With Your Vision I wish to see myself.
So that I may know myself
As You know me.

Psalm 149

In the midst of god's people,
Let us sing god new songs of praise!
Let us praise our creator,
Let us praise our fair and just ruler.
Let our praise of god so fill our being that we dance to
music not heard!
For god delights in us,
He crowns us in our poverty with victory,
So let us rejoice in the glory god gives us,
Let us joyfully feast of the lord's banquet.
Let our mouths give praise to god,
And our outstreatched arms gather in god's poor,
And so our works of justice and charity
Will be a rebuke to the self satisfied and self
enclosed.
God will trust us to bind up those who have bound up
others,
God will trust us to make powerless the powerful,
And to enact god's just judgments in all things.
Such is the glory god gives to his faithful people.
So let us shout
Hallelulia!

San Francesco A Rippa

If you want to know me,
Look at where my feet took me:
Before the pope
Seated in Lateran splendor,
Plush with pomp and power.
But to rest and laugh
And spend the night,
My feet carry me to the river's others side,
Where poor and sick,
And Jew remain.
It's to them
I am brother,
Sister,
Mother.

Second Guessing Yesterday

Second guessing yesterday
Is like a thief that robs one of the joy of today
And like a roaring beast
That makes one fearful of tomorrow.

Some Will be Running

Some will be running,
Swept along by the Wind;
Some will be marching triumphantly.
Some will be carried,
Still others will dance while singing a Triune Tune;
And I will be satisfied
To be counted among those,
Who under the feathery weight of grace,
Simply stumble their way through heaven's gates.

The Dark Parts

Though
We focus on the star,
It's in the night
That Christ was born.
So
It's not in the soul's light side,
Bright side
Where Christ appears,
But deep within the dark
Parts of our sin wounded heart.

The Great Impossibility

The great impossibility:
Mortals reaching heaven.
So God bent low
To become one of us
In the loving act of the great letting go,
To wrap us in Divinity.

The Pearl

Sometimes
I see myself
As a tiny grain of sand,
An irritant
On the tender heart of God.
And I wait
For grace to change me into a pearl.

The Poet

The poet,
As theologian,
Uses words to vivify,
The one mystery
Beyond all words.
But to the practiced eye,
It is in the spaces
Between the letters,
The spaces   between
The   words,
Thatmystery
Sings
silence
And resides.

The Prayer of Manasseh

The Prayer of Manasseh (from the Apocrypha)
O God,
Who created the universe through Your Word,
And by Your Breath gave us life;
Lord of our ancestors,
Before You all creation quivers with awe
Because of Your Abiding Presence and Loving Power.
You are for us abundant Mercy, Kindness, Love,
The likes of which we cannot imagine.
You are for us Eternal Compassion and Patience.
Though we deserve to be punished,
You do not hold out a fist, but rather a Loving Hand.
Because You are Goodness Itself,
You Give to the sinner not punishment, but
Forgiveness
So that we might accept Your gift of salvation through
a penitent faith.
So now I who sit among the ashes and ruin of what I
have done without You,
And name my vices and sins,
Not because I am courageous,
But because I have tasted Your great goodness.
Therefore, I make this prayer:
Forgive me Lord,
For what I have done and what I have failed to do.
Don't let my sin shroud me in guilt and shame;
Don't let death have the last word.

You O God are with those who repent,
You O God can create me anew.
Though unworthy, You love me,
And Your love will save me.
You Who are Love,
Invite me to join in the singing of creation's unending
song of praise.
You Who Are Love reach through the cosmos,
And create a home in me.
(based on the Song of Manasseh)

The Solemnity of the Ascension 2016

As you disappeared from human view,
To take your place in the heavenly heart of the
Church,
Christ raised a hand as if to say,
"You are blessed,
Not cursed.
You are blessed,
Not forgotten.
You are blessed,
Not abandoned.
You are blessed,
Not alone.
You are blessed,
Not weakened.
You are blessed,
Not defeated."
I know what I was,
I know who I am,
And on this festal day,
I know what I too can be.

The Tree I Pass

The tree I pass
Once, twice, thrice
A day,
Dares me not to contemplate
That once unnoticed buds
Have almost overnight
Burst into bloom.
Or so it appears to me.
Petals of various shades of violet
Call,
Cry out,
Command:
See!
But more than see,
Understand.
God is a too often unnoticed bud
Waiting to bloom within each of us.

The Universe was Created for Christ

The universe was created for Christ,
The prophets foretold Christ,
The Baptist prepared the people for Christ,
Joseph legitimized Christ,
Mary gave birth to Christ,
Angels sang of Christ,
Magi sought Christ.
And what of us?
We are to be Christ.

There are days

There are days
When I blame You, my God
For Self-Gift given yet soon withdrawn.
A God-Who-Is
Close and closer still;
BEING ever nearer,
Who doesn't always stay.
But now,
Through sixty year old eyes,
I begin to see that all the flight is mine.
It's I,
Not You,
Who turns and quickly runs away.

There will be weeping

There will be weeping
And gnashing of teeth.
Arbitrary punctuation
Makes this mine.
But I wonder,
If my eyes don't weep here,
And my teeth not gnash,
How can I in the infinite then?
So in my theology,
My best guess of what's to come,
It is YOU who weep and gnash,
All the while crying out,
"For you, what more could I have done?"

Though You Lead Me Forward

Though You lead me forward,
I like Lot's wife,
Look back and
Sigh
Over all I've left behind.
Yet,
You give me more
Than any one can promise
Or steal away.
(Genesis 19: 26)

Tis Grace To Be

'Tis grace to be
Created
Cracked,
To be at home in poverty
And embrace our human frailty.
Since
You our Christ
Fill all our need
In Your divine humanity.

Three Short Poems

I.
Dreams
Leave feelings
To be considered…
Or if you will,
Grist
For reflection.

II.
God is the Hostess of the ball:
Now a wall- flower
Patiently waiting for
Her invitation to
Dance.

III.
There is
Nothing more beautiful than
An opened
Church door.

Today

Today
I prayed,
"Meet me half way, O Lord."
And God
Replied,
"How can I meet you half way
When I am always already with you?"

Two Short Poems

I.
Grace overwhelms me.
Yet
I do not drown.
I soar!

II.
Excuses for my own faults
Fall so easily off my tongue.
While forgiveness
Sits like a lump in my throat.

When Your Wind Blows

When Your Wind blows
Trees sway their arms in a holy hula,
Grasses and flowers nod their heads to the divine
unheard beat.
Birds soar and jest on thermal jets;
Fallen leaves join together
Swirling multi-colored circles on the ground,
While even dust devils seem to jump and prance for
joy.
Oh if only the stones and I would join in the dance.

Words of War

Words of war
Are too easily shouted
Infecting a noble nationalism
With fevered zeal and xenophobia.
Words of war
Provoke clenched fists
While military might tramples meekness.
Words of war
Strips the other of our common humanity
While we too become something less than human.
Words of war
Demand plowshares be turned into guns
And worse,
The bodies and blood of our youth.
Words of war
Carve coffins and urns for our dead
And the stillborn dreams of those left living.
So let words of war be used sparingly
Or better yet,
Never said.

What the Robins Teach Us

In the early hours
Of a chilly Sunday morning,
Amid the false privacy of some low hanging branches,
I spied two robins mating.
The female seemingly ambivalent
Or unaware
Of all the attention being paid her.

Where does the grace of faith reside?

Where does the grace of faith reside?
For some, faith crowns the head,
Others discover
Faith nests within the shattered and broken heart,
Or moves the callused hand.
For me,
Faith moves my feet
Taking me to a place I'd rather not go.

ABOUT THE AUTHOR

Fr. Steve K., OFM is a Franciscan parish priest.

Made in the USA
Columbia, SC
27 July 2020